# Walking Out the Bible in Our Daily Lives

# The Beginning

# Walking Out the Bible in Our Daily Lives

## The Beginning

## E. E. Campbell

REDHAWK
PUBLICATIONS

Walking Out the Bible In Our Daily Lives: The Beginning

Copyright © 2024 E. E. Campbell

ISBN: 978-1-959346-63-0 (Paperback)

Library of Congress Control Number: 2024000000

Book Cover Design: Melanie Johnson Zimmermann

Book Interior Design: Robert T Canipe

Printed  in the United States of America.

First printing edition: 2024.

Redhawk Publications

The Catawba Valley Community College Press

2550 Hwy 70 SE

Hickory NC 28602

https://redhawkpublications.com

# Contents

# Foreword

I am thankful for my relationship with my Savior, Jesus, and His directing me to write this book. I was not going to start writing books with a Biblical basis. I would start with light writing since I have written a few short stories. Still, God had other plans, directed by transitioning my wife Karen Campbell on January 11, 2024, from her Earthly suit and her welcoming into her Heavenly home with Jesus.

For many years, I thought people talked about the Bible but did not live it. This book is called *Walking Out the Bible in Our Daily Lives: The Beginning.*

I am uncertain about the number of books that will be part of this project that Jesus has guided me to initiate. My aspiration is that Jesus will find favor in how I handle this book, and I envision Karen smiling from Heaven as well. My hope is that readers will be able to discern how to translate their beliefs from the Bible into their daily lives. I do not intend for this to be an exhaustive compilation of Biblical principles, nor a comprehensive guide on how everyone can incorporate the Bible into their daily lives. The majority of scripture references in this book will be from the King James Version (KJV), unless otherwise specified. My prayer is that every reader will allow the Holy Spirit to guide their hearts and lives, and they will, as my pastor says, 'connect the dots in their lives.'

May God be glorified and honored through the writing of this book, and may His work in every person's life be magnified through this book. It was His leading that brought me to author this book. I had never conceived of a book like this before God directed me to undertake this project. He has not allowed me to abandon this idea. Only God knows the number of books or the intervals between them. May He be glorified in all of this, and may He, as He deems fit, transform many lives through this book.

# Introduction

Our journey through the Bible, a profound exploration of Biblical principles, is not a mere casual stroll. It's a purposeful expedition, much like a planned trip in a car, on a plane, or on a boat. And just as any journey has a starting and end point, so does ours. We embark from the very beginning, as the book's subtitle suggests, to fully immerse ourselves in the wisdom of the Scriptures.

The beginning of this journey starts with who God is and how everything is dependent on him. This means that we will determine many truths about Him and some key facts about our world.

Our understanding of God is a lifelong pursuit, a continuous journey of discovery. As I mentioned in the foreword, this book is not an exhaustive study of God. Such a task would be monumental, requiring extensive time, effort, and resources. Even a lifetime of learning would not unveil all there is to know about Him. But it's in this ongoing quest that we find the true essence of our faith.

As we begin this dive into the Bible and its Biblical principles, we start with a question that Jesus asked his disciples: "Who do you say that I am?" found in Matthew 16.15. Which says, "He saith unto them, 'But who say ye that I am?'" We will not be able to unpack this question fully, but hopefully, we can unpack enough to understand who God is and how we fit into His world.

By answering the above question, we will have to learn things about our world and humanity.

As we conclude this first book, my aspiration is for you to have experienced a profound transformation in your faith. I hope that you have not only deepened your understanding of God but also begun to live out your faith in your daily life. If this hasn't been the case, I still hope that you have gleaned insights about God that have brought you closer to a personal relationship with Him. The journey continues, and I'm excited to accompany you on this path.

If either of the situations stated above were to happen in your life, then I have done my purpose in writing this book and the others that will follow. I hope that you will enjoy the journey through the Bible as I will as I write this book.

# Chapter 1

# Who God is Not

Before delving into the profound exploration of God's true nature, it's crucial to first dispel some common misconceptions. For instance, some may envision Him as a distant cosmic figure, merely reacting to our actions and influencing nature. This view, however, underestimates His personal interaction with humanity, a fundamental aspect of His nature that we must fully grasp. Our aim is to enlighten and correct these misconceptions, paving the way for a clearer understanding of God's true nature.

One other thought is that He is a "Heavenly Santa," who is in Heaven only to give us what we want as we ask. This thinking is that He wants to make us happy by simply giving us what we demand of Him, just like Santa Claus. The problem with this idea is that He is doing something other than waiting for us to ask Him something. Suppose we are good enough and doing what is good for us and His will. We will get what we ask of God no matter what it is. Thinking of Him in either of these ideas is much smaller than He. We lose with both thought processes. There are many different wrong approaches to who He is. We will examine a couple of other methods before examining who God is.

Another approach is God as a grandfather or parent in Heaven or who does not care about us unless it is to punish us for doing something wrong. With this idea, we are victims of a cosmic being who wants to crush us for doing wrong. The picture here is the old arcade game of "Whack-a-mole." When the person is playing, waiting for the mole to pop up so they can use a hammer to bop it, He looks like an angry grandfather or parent who only wants to punish his children or grandchildren.

The idea is that God created everything and then took His hand and mind off of it, leaving us to try to live in the world on our strength, knowledge, and ability. This mindset says we must do our best; whatever happens is just luck or chance. It also claims that we control this world and can make it what we want.

Another option is that there is no God or cosmic being, and everything happens by chance. There is no rhyme or reason about anything. This is problematic because everything will always be chaotic in this ideology. This is also called the "big bang." However, there is too much order in this creation to be able to buy that thought in any way.

People believe that God was created and has a starting and end point. For this to be true, we should find something in science that shows where His existence began and a possible endpoint.

While we could continue to dissect these misconceptions, it's crucial to shift our focus to the Bible and its teachings about God. This will serve as a sturdy foundation for our journey through the scriptures. Your active involvement in this process is not just encouraged, but essential. So, let's embark on our quest to understand who God truly is and what that understanding means for each of us.

# Chapter 1 at a glance:

- *The text discusses common misconceptions about God, such as envisioning Him as a distant figure only reacting to our actions, a "Heavenly Santa" fulfilling our every wish, or an indifferent cosmic force.*

- *Another misconception is viewing God as either a punishing figure or as having detached Himself from creation, leaving humanity to fend for itself.*

- *The text emphasizes the importance of shifting focus to the Bible and its teachings about God to gain a clearer understanding of His nature, encouraging active involvement in the process.*

# Chapter 1 Discussion Questions

# *No God*

1) Does it make sense now why there being no God is not good?

2) Does the existence of nature itself show us that He exists?

3) Does it make sense that we can never find God's start or end, and does it help you want to see God's traits?

# Chapter 2

# No Beginning or Ending

Now, we are going to look at who God is. The first thing that we need to explore about God is his existence. That means we will look at His starting point and discuss His possible endpoint.

What do we know about the starting point of God? Is there a point in time that He started or was created? The Bible does tell us a lot about this question. Genesis 1.1 states:

*"In the Beginning, God created the Heaven and the Earth."*

This makes the ideology that everything we know about Heaven and Earth started with God. This would mean that He had no starting point of His existence. It would assume that God has always existed. An eternal existence does not support the idea of a "Big Bang." We will look at this idea of creation later in this book's chapter.

Through the Bible, we find that His existence has always been. John 1.1 says,

*"In the beginning was the Word, and the Word was with God, and the Word was God."*

Once again, He was at the beginning of everything we know. If God was at the beginning of everything, it is only logical to assume that He had no beginning or that there is no possible end point for Him. This concept is challenging for us to wrap our minds around.

With all of the scientific developments, we should have found some evidence that showed where God started. If this is true, we must believe He was in Genesis 0.0. You will not see this in the Bible because there is no zero chapter of Genesis. So, let us look at other facts about what it means for God not to have a beginning or an ending.

In Exodus, God commissions Moses to take the Children of Israel out of bondage in Egypt. Moses asked the voice talking to him out of the bush who he should say was sending him to deliver God's people out of bondage. Exodus 3 says in verse fourteen,

*"And God said unto Moses, I am that I am: and he said, Thus shalt thou say unto the children of Israel, I am hath sent me unto you."*

I am telling you this to look at one other thing that would show that God has always existed.

The statement "I am that I am" shows us once again that He has always existed. It is hard to understand that God has always existed because modern science wants us to see an existence that started from gases that no one can explain where they came from and that everything on this Earth has just evolved and will continue until it can no longer. That means that we must decide which ideology we are going to believe and which one makes sense in our lives.

If we decide that what the Bible says about God is accurate, we must discuss Him more. God's existence means we must discuss whether there is any way to show He is not contained in time. The best Biblical evidence is in 2 Peter 3.8:

*"But, beloved, be not ignorant of this one thing, that one day is with the Lord as a thousand years and a thousand years as one day."*

Some people would want to use this to support the idea of the accident of gases coming from the unknown and evolution happening as a possibility. If the Bible is true, He is not confined to time. Now that we have looked at the facts discussed in the Bible, we can see how this looks.

The people who say there must be a beginning to the God of the Bible have a challenging task before them. To determine that God has a beginning, they must show where that beginning is. To do this a person must be able to go to the end or beginning of the universe. If a person could do that, that person would have to become God or a god to accomplish this task. It is hard to even think about accomplishing such a task.

It takes faith to find ourselves on either side of God's position. However, if a person takes the Bible's truth as their guide, there is hope that everything in this world must have a bigger purpose in God's mind for our humanity and creation.

As we look at everything going on in this world, I hope there is a reason for the good and the bad that happens in our world. An example of this would be everything I have faced in my life. The hardest thing up to this point would be the loss of my wife Karen on January 11, 2024.

My hope up to this point is that you will understand that God has no beginning or end, giving you hope that nothing in life happens without purpose and that our lives have a small part in God's bigger plan. To show this in my life would be to show that God used Karen's death to examine Biblical principles in my life and those who read this book.

This is the first Biblical principle that we must understand if we are to understand the other principles in this book and the one that will follow.

The next principle we will examine in the next chapter is God's creation of everything in our world.

# Chapter 2 at a glance:

- *The text explores the concept of God's existence, arguing that God has always existed and has no beginning or end.*

- *It discusses biblical evidence supporting the idea that God is not confined by time.*

- *The author expresses hope that understanding God's timeless existence can bring purpose to both the good and bad experiences in life.*

# Chapter 2 Discussion Questions

# *No Beginning or Ending*

1) After reading this chapter, can you see that God is not contained in time and how important that is in the more significant understanding of our world?

2) What are your thoughts on the Big Bang theory versus God creating everything now?

3) Has this exploration ignited a fervent desire within you to delve deeper into the understanding of God?

# Chapter 3

# Creator

As we look at the world we live in, we must deal with the thought of how all we see came into existence. The idea is that gases come out of nowhere combined and explode, resulting in all we see. We can see everything and decide that someone must have created everything we see.

With the first idea, we must determine the origin of the gases, which would be impossible. The second idea is that out of chaos, we have such a beautiful world that we get to live in and enjoy. The world is so detailed that there had to be more to it than gases coming out of nowhere and producing this awesome world that we live in.

There has to be a person or more extraordinary being in all that we see and enjoy in our world. It is like looking at a very detailed watch in a jewelry store and realizing that someone must have put all their thoughts and energy into creating it. We would never think that the watch's parts just appeared and came together, making the watch we are looking at in the store.

If the statement above is true, it is logical that a person or more extraordinary being has to create everything we see and know as our world. That would be God, who made everything we see and know.

To understand how He was able to design everything that we see and enjoy, we must quickly revisit a few details mentioned in Chapter 2. The fact that God has always existed and is not confined to time means He is perfect for being the creator of all we know.

He created everything that we know and can see by looking at a few scriptures that show us how everything came into existence. In Genesis, we have the statement,

*"In the beginning, God created the* Heaven *and the* Earth.*"*

This is found in Genesis 1.1. It is impressive to see what is detailed in this statement—the Heaven where He and all the Heavenly beings dwell and where we can potentially live someday. We will look at the potential of living in Heaven with God and His Heavenly host in a later chapter in more detail. Amazingly, God created Heaven, which we cannot see with our natural eyes.

Now, we can look at the Earth that He created. When we look at the Earth, it is incredible itself. We see that the Earth was formless, and the Bible says,

*"...and the Earth was without form and void, and darkness was upon the face of the deep. And the Spirit of God moved upon the face of the waters."*

This is found in verse 2 of Genesis 1 of the scripture. We will look at the idea of the Spirit of God in detail in a later chapter.

Let's try to unpack what this verse tells us about the Earth we love. It shows us that God started with nothing, and now we have what we see and enjoy today. It is amazing that He started with nothing and created all that we see. How could He take nothing and create everything? This verse also tells us that there was nothing but darkness on the Earth.

As we read further in Genesis 1, we will discover how

He took care of the darkness on Earth in the beginning. We see that God spoke, let there be light, and we had light as we know it today. It is incredible that at His word light appeared simply by His request. After He created light, God looked at it and saw it was good.

Next, we see that God divided the light from the darkness. He called the light Day and the darkness Night. This was done by speaking it into existence.

After He created the Night and Day, He created time as we know it today. The scripture says, "And God called him light Day, and the darkness he called Night. And the evening and the morning were the first Day." Amazingly, He did this in a 24-hour time frame.

We see that Heaven in Genesis also refers to the Universe we know today. He created the Universe and all its lights, the moon, the Sun, and the stars. It is fantastic to understand that God created everything we know by saying a word. He said it was good as He finished each part of the creation. This is hard to wrap our minds around, but it is true.

He also created humanity. This is more important than all of creation because God formed us with His hands and breathed life into us. After He finished all of creation, God said it was very good. We can find this statement in Genesis 1:31. This verse also tells us that He did all of this in six days. He also rested to give us the principle of taking one Day to rest. This will be discussed in a later book in this series. This is mind-blowing.

We see that Adam, the first man, could not find a match when God created man. This could have been better. He took man, his first human, removed one of his ribs, and made His second human called woman. Then, He called them Adam and Eve. Readers can find this in Genesis 2.

We see that God created the first marriage of all time. The statement in scripture exemplifies this,

*"Therefore shall a man leave his father and his mother, and shall cleave unto his wife: and they shall be one flesh."*

This is found in Genesis 2.24. We will look at the Biblical principle of marriage in one of the other books in this series. In a later chapter, we will examine man and our problem in God's creation. I could go on forever about God as creator, but we must consider how to put this into our lives daily.

This is a lot of information to take into our minds and then apply to our lives. I will show you one way to try to do this.

When we look at the beauty of the Earth, it should shock us into awe of all that God created. Just looking at the mountains and the beauty that is found in looking at the mountains, or being on a mountain top and looking at everything from there and knowing that we have oxygen to be that high in the air and looking down on everything in the valley below. Being in a valley and seeing all of the flowers in all of their splendor and knowing that they are that pretty because God spoke them into existence should make us almost faint with all the splendor of the flowers. This could be said of all of the creations from the Universe, stars, moons, suns, and beyond.

The Earth is the third planet from the Sun because if we were any closer to the Sun, we would burn up, and if we were any farther away, we would freeze to death. Just thinking about this should show us God's handiwork in creation.

Looking at humanity, we see we have so many parts that make up our bodies. The fact that all of the parts work together as they should make us thankful that He knew what He was doing in our creation. Doctors seem to learn more about our bodies than they had no clue about, which also shows us God is awesome in how He designed us.

The last thing to look at is God creating marriage. In our world, we see many people who take the fact of being married for granted. We see God created marriage, and we should cherish our marriage. God knew what He was doing in all of creation, including marriage. This is all amazing.

The biblical principle of God as a creator should cause us to enjoy our lives in His creation and praise Him for all that we have because of His creative design.

We will look at God being all-powerful in the next chapter.

# Chapter 3 at a glance

- *The text discusses the idea that a higher being, such as God, created everything we see and know in the world, including the heavens, the earth, and humanity.*

- *It explores the concept of creation as described in the book of Genesis, emphasizing that God created the universe and all living beings, including the first man and woman, Adam and Eve.*

- *The text also mentions the significance of God's creation of marriage and highlights the principle of rest, as well as the potential for living in Heaven with God and His Heavenly host.*

# Chapter 3 Discussion Questions

# *Creator*

1) Can you see how God is the creator of all of our world as we can see it?

2) How does knowing He is the creator change your thoughts about God now?

# Chapter 4

# Omnipotent God

In the previous chapter of this journey through the Bible to uncover its principles, we discovered that God is the creator and not contained in time.

To better understand Him as a creator, we have to put the principle of not being contained in time with the fact that He is Omnipotent as well.

What does the word *omnipotent* mean? It means that God has all power, and there is nothing that He cannot do.

We saw a great example of this in the last chapter because God only had to speak it, which happened in creation. It is hard to believe that just speaking would allow for all creation that we see and enjoy could be done.

He took his hands and made humanity. Why did God not speak creation into existence until He got to humanity? He did this to show that He can speak things into existence, and the creator could also use His hands to create humankind.

All of this is found in the Bible's first two chapters of Genesis, but you might be saying, is there any other proof found in the scriptures that shows that He is all-powerful?

When we see the calling of Moses to lead the people of Israel out of bondage in Egypt, We know that He allowed a bush to be on fire but was not consumed by the fire that was all around the bush. Exodus 3.1 says,

*"And Moses said, I will now turn aside, and see this great sight, why the bush is not burnt."*

If we were Moses, this would have gotten our attention as well. This is another example found in the pages of God's Holy Word, the Bible.

We see three young Hebrews, Shadrach, Meshach, and Abed-Nego, mentioned in the Bible who refused to worship King Nebuchadnezzar and make an image of him. Nebuchadnezzar demanded that the people in Babylon hear all kinds of music. All were to bow down to his image, and anyone who did not bow down would be thrown into a fire furnace. These young Hebrew men refused to bow down to the image, which made Nebuchadnezzar so mad that he ordered the furnace to be heated seven times hotter than ever. The king had his best men bind the young men and throw them into the furnace, and the men throwing them into the furnace were consumed by the furnace's fire. The Hebrew men fell into the furnace. When King Nebuchadnezzar investigated the furnace, he saw four men walking around in the furnace. His people were asked if three men were thrown into the furnace. They confirmed that only three were put into the furnace, and He said, "I see four men walking around in the furnace, and one looked like a son of God. When three Hebrew men came out of the fire, the ropes were gone, but they were not burned, and there was no smell of the smoke from the fire. This is found in Daniel chapter 3 of the Bible.

This shows that God has enough power to protect His children from anything that might try to hurt them. The scripture also tells us nothing can stand against us if God is for us. This can be found in Romans 8.31 of the scriptures.

We also have the story in the Gospels: Matthew, Mark, Luke, and John, two different accounts of Jesus, the Son of God, feeding four and five thousand men, not including women and children, which will be looked at in the next chapter of this book. We see here that God can take a little bit of food and make it to feed this big group of people who have leftovers. This is just one more way we see that God is all-powerful.

The one other example we will examine to show God's omnipotence will also be found in the gospels. Jesus and His disciples got into a boat and traveled to the other side. A colossal storm started while they journeyed to the other side of the Sea of Galilee. The disciples were experienced fishermen, and they were scared for their lives. They woke Jesus, who was at the bottom of the boat asleep, and He spoke to the storm, and the storm stopped. Matthew 8.26 states,

*"And he saith unto them, Why are ye fearful, O ye of little faith? Then he arose and rebuked the winds and the sea, and there was a great calm."*

This shows that God created everything and that it must obey his powerful voice after creating everything.

The last example to show that God is powerful would be the story of Lazarus, found in John 11. After he had been dead for four days, Jesus came to the scene. He says Lazarus come forth, and Lazarus comes out of the grave. We see that His power is even greater than death.

Now that we have examined all the evidence of God's omnipotence, it is important to see how this can be applied to our daily lives.

As Christians, we must understand that we are safe because we are children of God. Our safety is dependent on our Savior's being all-powerful, and we can call out to Him when we are in trouble. God can come to our aid just like He did in the scriptures. This should be a major hope for us as Christians.

Even if we were to die, we can go to Heaven due to the fact of His power overcoming death when Jesus died on the cross for our sins.

If you are not a Christian, His power should give you a fear of God that can lead to a personal relationship with Him. One of the other books in this series will examine this in more detail.

We will look at the trinity of God, in the next chapter.

# Chapter 4 at a glance

- *The text discusses the omnipotence of God, emphasizing that He has all power and can do anything.*

- *It provides several examples from the Bible to illustrate God's omnipotence, such as the creation story, the story of the fiery furnace, Jesus feeding thousands, calming the storm, and raising Lazarus from the dead.*

- *The text highlights that as Christians, we can find hope and security in God's omnipotence, as His power extends to protecting and guiding us in our daily lives.*

# Chapter 4

## *Omnipotent God*

1) After reading this chapter, can you see how God is Omnipotent?

2) Does that help you see how He created the whole creation and time now?

3) What are your thoughts about God after reading this chapter?

# Chapter 5

# Trinity

We will now look at the fact that God is a trinity. Which means that He is three but one. This isn't easy to understand because our minds cannot wrap around the thought. I will give us some insight into this fact about Him.

We will start with the fact that God is Heavenly Father in Heaven. This can be seen in several places in the Word of God, the Bible.

Let's get started. When Jesus was on Earth, His disciples asked him how to pray. He told them to start the prayer by saying, "Our Father, who art in Heaven." This shows us that God is three in one because Jesus refers to God as His Father in Heaven. Jesus tells His disciples,

*"Your Father knows what you need before you ask Him."*

This can be found in Matthew 6.8-9, which says,

*"Be not ye, therefore, like unto them: for your Father knoweth what things ye need of before ye ask Him."*

It continues,

*"After this manner therefore pray ye: Our father which art in heaven, Hallowed be thy name."*

In another passage, we see Jesus talk about God as Heavenly Father. We see this when He tells those around Him that He cannot do anything unless He sees the Father doing something here, and He will join His Father in the action.

*"But Jesus answered them, My Father worketh hitherto, and I work."*

This is found in John 5.17. He continues by saying,

*"Then answered Jesus and said unto them, Verily, verily, I say unto you, The Son can do nothing of himself, but what he seeth the Father do: for what things soever he doeth, these also doeth the Son likewise."*

These are just two examples of God the Father found in the Bible.

Now, we will look at Jesus as one part of the Godhead and how the scripture shows Jesus as the second person of the Godhead.

In the book of John, we can see this very quickly as John 1.1 states,

*"In the beginning was the Word, and the Word was with God, and the Word was God."*

This passage says in the beginning was the Word. The word "Word" is referring to Jesus. We see that Jesus was there in the beginning. The beginning talks about the beginning of the World as we know it today. It also tells us that Jesus and God the Father are one.

In the same passage, we see another example of Jesus as the Godhead. John 1.14 says,

*"And the Word was made Flesh, and dwelt among us, (and we beheld his glory, the glory as of the only begotten of the Father,) full of grace and truth."*

In this verse, we see that Jesus is God just as much as God the Father is.

The last thing about Jesus in this chapter is that He says that if you have seen the Son, you have seen the Father. Jesus also makes it clear in the passage of the Bible once again that They are one. John 14.8-11 says,

*"Philip saith unto him, Lord, show us the Father, and it sufficeth us. Jesus saith unto him, Have I been so long with you, and yet hast thou not known me, Philip? He that hath seen me hath seen the Father; and how sayest thou then, Show us the Father?*

*"Believest thou not that I am in the Father, and the Father in me? The words that I speak not of myself: but the Father that dwelleth in me, he doeth the works. Believe me that I am in the Father, and the Father in me: or else believe me for the very works' sake."*

I could go on forever about how Jesus is in the second part of the Godhead, but it is time to look at the last part.

The last part of the Godhead we will look at is the Holy Spirit. In Genesis 1, we see the Spirit at work in the creation of the wonderful World that we live in. It shows the Spirit working and moving in creation.

*"And the Earth was without form and void, and darkness was upon the face of the deep. And the Spirit of God moved upon the face of the waters."*

This shows that the Spirit was involved in the creation we know. It is fantastic to see how the whole Godhead was involved in everything from the beginning.

We see that the Spirit was also involved in the creation of man. Genesis 1.26 states,

*"And God said, Let us make man in our image, after our likeness: and let them have dominion over the fish of the air, and over every creeping thing that creepeth upon the earth."*

This shows us just how God created everything.

To continue discussing the Spirit, we must examine who He is and what He is not.

Many people think that the Spirit is a force on Earth that works in our lives, and that is all the Spirit is. They look at the Spirit like Star Wars. May the Spirit be with you. It is unbelievable to think that the third person of the Godhead is just a force.

We will examine the Bible for what it says about the Spirit so that we can have the truth about the Spirit.

The Spirit is a person of the Godhead. We can see this in many different passages in the scripture. The first one we see is that He can be lied to about things just like an average person. We see this can be found in The Book of Acts. The church was beginning, and followers of Christ were selling possessions and giving it to the church to provide for the needs of the early church. A husband and a wife sold their property; however, they decided to keep a portion for themselves. They proceeded to tell the disciples that what they were giving them was the sale of the property in full. The disciples confronted them, and God told the disciples the husband and wife were lying. The disciples asked them why they lied to the Holy Spirit, and the two fell dead. This shows the personal traits of the Spirit, three persons of the Godhead.

We see that He can be grieved just like any other person. Ephesians 4.30 states,

*"And grieve not the holy Spirit of God, whereby ye are sealed unto the day of redemption."*

We see that the Spirit is a person like Jesus and the Father. All three are needed in creation and in our lives.

We need to understand that the Father is a person who operates in this World and the lives of Christians today. He is the real God, not a god, and controls everything in our World.

Jesus is important. Without realizing that, His work of Salvation in humanity, no person would have the opportunity to have a personal relationship with God through Jesus and an opportunity to live in Heaven forever. We will discuss this in more detail in the next book in this series, as the section of this book is called a *personal* relationship with God.

The Spirit shows people they need Jesus and guides us in our lives as Children of God. As stated above, we will get more details about this in our next book and a special section of this book.

Even though each person of the Godhead has a role in our lives, they are also one, and the best way to see this is to look at our own bodies, which are created in God's image.

Our skin aims to protect our bones, blood vessels, and other organs, but skin functioning without the different parts of our bodies would not be good. It must be part of the whole of our bodies.

Our skeletal system gives us form and the ability to walk, talk, and move. The bones working alone could accomplish little.

The respiratory system gives us the ability to breathe. If we did not breathe, we would not be alive because our bodies need oxygen for the other parts of the body to function properly.

As we can see, the Trinity of the Godhead is a must. However, we must look at each one separately in order to understand its functions. Just like we need all of our body systems to make us complete and have to look at each separately to understand how they work, I hope this helps you know the Trinity.

As we understand the Trinity, we can live a proper Christian life. The Father tells the Spirit to convict us of our sins and our need for Jesus as our savior. Jesus paid the price for our sins and gave us the ability to have Salvation. Once we are children of God, the Spirit works to show us how to live the Christian life and convicts us when we go astray.

This will help you live a better life in Jesus by helping you understand the Trinity. If you are not a Christian, this will inspire you to learn how to become one.

# Chapter 5 at a glance

- *The text discusses the concept of the Holy Trinity, explaining that God is three in one - the Heavenly Father, Jesus, and the Holy Spirit, as depicted in the Bible.*

- *It explores the biblical references to each person of the Godhead, emphasizing Jesus as the second person of the Trinity and the Holy Spirit's role in creation and in the lives of believers.*

- *The text emphasizes the personhood of the Holy Spirit and refutes the misconception that the Holy Spirit is merely a force, highlighting biblical passages that support the Spirit's unique status as a person of the Godhead.*

# Chapter 5 Discussion Questions

## *Trinity*

1) Do you understand the Trinity of God better now that you have read this chapter?

2) Do you see how each part of the Trinity is vital?

3) Does the newfound knowledge about the trinity trait of God bring you joy and a sense of spiritual enrichment?

# Chapter 6

# Man

Now, we will look at God's most significant Creation and His biggest problem.

However, God spoke everything into existence; He took the time to create us with His hands. This amazes me since everything else in Creation was just spoken into existence. It tells me that humanity was unique enough for Him to take the time to create us personally.

Not only did He create humanity with His own hands, but He also breathed life into us. Everything else in Creation had life in it as spoken into existence. We have the life of God himself breathed into us. This means that we were more than just part of Creation; we have a crucial role in His Creation.

We were also created in the likeness of the Godhead, meaning we are at the top of all Creation. Being at the top of God's Creation means we have more responsibility than anything else created, period. This is amazing and scary at the same time.

We know that only after we were created did God make a different statement from the rest of Creation. When He created all the Creation and looked at what He had made, He said that it was good, but God looked at us after creating us and said, "It was perfect." All of this is found in Genesis chapter 1.

He also commanded us to have dominion over all the rest of Creation. This was a very massive command. We will see that it is tough for us to obey. We will look more at this in the next book of this series.

We can reason, but we need the rest of Creation to have the ability to do this in any way. We have intelligent animals; however, they can only react to things around them. The animals cannot reason why they acted the way they did in a situation in Creation, but we, as humanity, can.

We were told we could eat everything except one tree in the Garden of Eden. This sounds good, but we will find out later that it is more challenging than it sounds. I am glad that we can find out all about this in the Bible's first three chapters of Genesis.

Adam was privileged to provide names for all of Earth's animals. He gave all the animals the names that we call animals today. This also includes dinosaurs; I say this because God only created everything once. I am going to take a quick detour. Some believe there are two different creation accounts, known as the gap theory. This is how they try to justify Creation and evolution together. This idea is that He created dinosaurs, which are being destroyed and starting over again in which we were created. I only bring this up because Adam was responsible for naming all Creation.

In this task, Adam, God, wanted to see if any Creation could be his companion. He saw that nothing in the Creation was suitable for him, and this caused God to say, "This is not good." It is the only time in all of Creation that God used that phrase.

He wanted to fix this situation with Adam. He caused a deep sleep to come on Adam, took the rib from Adam, and created the other human, Eve. This restored Creation to be good.

We were then given the institution of marriage and the task of filling the whole Earth with more humans. This was the start of humanity. We will see later that this would go bad at one point in our history and must be fixed.

I could go on forever about what man was in the Creation, but I want to take the time to look at a few things that we can do as God's highest-created beings.

We have the opportunity to worship and praise God for all that He does in our lives. We get to create things with our hands and think freely for ourselves. The ability to choose for ourselves is great, but later, we will see that this is a big problem.

# Chapter 6 at a glance

- *Humanity was created uniquely by God's hands and was given the breath of life, making humans distinct from the rest of Creation.*

- *Humans were created in the likeness of the Godhead, with the responsibility of having dominion over all other creations.*

- *Adam was created as the first human, and Eve was later created from his rib, marking the beginning of humanity and the institution of marriage.*

# Chapter 6 Discussion Questions

# *Man*

1) Can you see how humanity is unique in all of God's creation?

2) Isn't it a marvel that we, unlike the rest of creation, have the ability to reason and create?

3) Are you interested in discovering more about man, which we will find in the next book?

# Chapter 7

# Walking Out the Bible

We have examined several different Biblical principles and some ways to live them out in our lives. We will apply all of the principles discussed so that they are lived out or worked out in our lives.

The first principle we examined was the fact that God is not contained in time. In fact, He created time as we know it now.

As believers, this should give us hope that He can see everything going on in our lives and that God knows everything in our lives. This is important for the Christian because God is always ready to work in our lives to accomplish His will. He knows when we are going to not follow His will and just how this will affect our lives. He is ready for us to come back when we stray from Him.

If we are not believers, He knows what needs to happen in our lives to get us to come to Him and receive a personal relationship with Him through Jesus. Having this relationship with God is great for anyone to have working in their life.

We are realizing that God created everything in the world. It should give us hope that He can handle and control everything in our lives since God made it all from the start. When we are going through something medically, it is fantastic to think that our God knows our bodies perfectly and can give doctors the knowledge to see what is going on and how to deal with our medical issues. If no doctor has no clue what is going on with us, it is comforting to know that our God knows and can fix it Himself without using the medical system in our world.

In the last paragraph, we touched on one of God's other principles: He is all-powerful. How can this be lived out in our daily lives? Knowing that God is omnipotent, we can be assured that nothing we may face in this world can be handled if we lean on Him for all that we need, no matter what might come into our lives. God has the power to protect all His children from all harm that might come our way.

Knowing that God is a Tri-union is also suitable for us as believers. It means that the Godhead is working in our lives as one of the persons of the Trinity. This is important because understanding that you cannot have just one of the persons of the Trinity without the other. All of them were present in our creation. Each one has a part in our coming into a personal relationship with God because without all of them working in our salvation, it would not be able to happen in our lives. As we travel through our life journey, each one plays an integral part in getting us through some of the most challenging times in our lives. God is critical in the great happiness in our lives as well.

Humanity is the most important part of God's creation. We need to realize that we need to manage God's world in a way that pleases Him and honors Him in all things.

Being able to create and choose is a great privilege given to us by God. We can think and create all that comes to our minds. It can be great that we are not robots or even like the rest of creation, but it can and did cause big problems for us, which we will look at in the next book in this series.

Now, I will share a story to show you how all of this plays out in our lives.

Because God is not contained in time, He knew that I would give my life to Him at a very young age. I am glad that I gave my life to him at a young age. He knew that I would have some challenging times in my life and that I would need to deal with all of them. In 1991, I surrendered to the call to preach God's word, and my Savior determined that time. I had to deal with many challenges in the military, but God knew people would be praying for me, asking God to be with me. This was very much needed. On August 22, 2015, God gave me a great Godly partner and wife in Karen Campbell. We dealt with many things medically that He got us through in our marriage together. He even protected her from death in a car wreck in 2022. However, on January 11, 2024, God allowed her to come home to Heaven. He knew this would happen and how hard these last one hundred and forty-one days would be, but He knew His power would get me through all of this now and in the future.

I hope my brief life story demonstrates all the principles we have discussed in this book. May God use all this to strengthen your faith in Christ.

# Chapter 7 at a glance

- *God's omnipotence and omnipresence: God's ability to see everything going on in our lives, control everything, and protect his children from harm.*

- *The Tri-union nature of God: Understanding the roles of the Father, Son, and Holy Spirit in our lives and salvation.*

- *Human responsibility and privilege: Our responsibility to manage God's world in a way that honors Him, and the privilege of being able to create and choose.*

# Chapter 7 Discussion Questions

## *Walking out the Bible*

1)Now that you have seen all the principles of the Bible in this book and how to possibly live them out in your life, consider the potential for growth in your walk with God.

2) Has this journey filled you with hope?

3) If you do not have a relationship with God, does this make you want to keep learning about God so you can have a relationship with God?

# Chapter 8

# Personal Relationship with Christ

For us to have a personal relationship with Christ, we must discuss a few things.

First, we must realize we are sinners who cannot fix this problem. Romans 3.23 says,

*"For all have sinned and come short of the glory of God."*

This means that we all are in trouble, and there are consequences for our sins.

Second, we have to understand the consequences of our sins. It is death, and we cannot change this fact no matter what we do. Going to church or having Christian family members will not fix this. Romans 6.23 states,

*"For the wages of sin is death; but the gift of God is eternal life through Jesus Christ our Lord."*

Third, what is the gift of God that can give us eternal life? It is the death of Jesus on the cross for our sins. This is the only way to fix the spiritual death our sins caused us. John 3.16 says,

*"For God so loved the world, that he gave him only begotten Son, that whosoever believeth in him should not perish, but have everlasting life."*

Okay, how can I do this? All we have to do is believe that God gave himself for us and rose from the grave to give us life and hope. Romans 10.9 states,

*"That if thou shalt confess with thy mouth the Lord Jesus, and shalt believe in thine heart that God hath raised him from the death, thou shalt be saved."*

The next question for you is whether there is any reason why you would not want this relationship with the God of the universe. If you say no, let's look at what you must do.

All you must do is pray and acknowledge that you are a sinner and cannot save yourself. Ask God to forgive you of your sins and make Jesus the Lord and Savior of your life. This means giving everything in your life to God through Jesus.

I would also ask you to tell someone you know is a Christian or if you go to church somewhere. Please let your pastor know because this will make him happy to hear from you.

# Acknowledgments

I want to thank everyone who has made this book and the series of books possible.

I want to thank my Lord and Savior, Jesus Christ, because, without him, there is no way I would have started writing a Biblical Basis book as my first book as an author.

I must thank my grandmother, Rosie Smith, because she gave me the desire to study God's word. She talked about how important the Bible was and how important having a relationship with God through Jesus was.

I have to thank all of my family for those who showed me how great it was to be a Child of God. Thank all of my family who have encouraged me while writing this book.

My late wife Karen Campbell must be thanked because she always supported me and my following the Lord. I know she is in Heaven right now, but she has been cheering me on as I have written this book.

All of the pastors and teachers who have been instrumental in my growth as a Child of God have played a big part in making this book a reality. I also have to thank all of my church family for their support.

I want to thank all my English teachers for teaching me English and giving me the desire to write. This goes back to 6th grade through my time at CVCC as a student and Fruitland Baptist Bible Institute English teacher.

I am indebted to my friends and co-workers, who have been a source of encouragement and support throughout the writing process. Your belief in me and this project has been invaluable.

I am writing to express my gratitude to Redhawk Publications for their pivotal role in bringing this book to life. Their belief in my work and their willingness to publish it have been instrumental. I also extend a special thanks to Robert Canipe for his meticulous editing. Your support and efforts have made this book a reality.

# About the Author

 E. E. Campbell is a born-again Child of God who was called into the ministry as a pastor in 1991. In 2008, Campbell studied electronic and computer engineering at CVCC. He then attended Fruitland Baptist Bible Institute, where he studied and graduated with a degree in biblical studies.

Campbell married Karen Campbell on August 22, 2015. They were married for 8 years until she went home to Heaven on January 11, 2024.

God moved Campbell to write this book in February 2024. He lives and works in Hickory, NC

Made in the USA
Middletown, DE
20 November 2024